वांछास्थापन परं विजयते श्रीकृष्णसङ्कीर्तनम

नाम्नामकारि बहुधा निजसर्वशक्ति   नाम्नामक

स्त्रापिता नियमितः स्मरणे न कालः

एतादृशी तव कृपा भगवन्ममापि   भगवन्ममापि   नाम्नामकारिएतादृशी

न्नदुर्दैवमीदृशमिहाजनि नानुरागः तव भगवन्ममापि

प्रादपि सुनीचेन तरोरिव सहिष्णुना   सहिष्णुना   नाम्नमकारि तरोरपि

अमानिना मानदेन कीर्तनीयः सदा हरिः सदा   आनन्तान्यिक अमानिना

न धनं न जनं न सुन्दरीं कवितां वा जगदीश कामये   सदा हरिः   सत्रापिनान धन

कविता वा जगदीश कामये मम जन्मनीश्वरे भवताद्भक्तिर

मम जन्मनि जन्मनीश्वरे मा विषमे भवाम्बुधो   सदा हरिः मम जन्म

भवताद्भक्तिरहैतुकी त्वायिविषमे भवाम्बुधेम भवताद्भक्ति रहैतुकी भवनन्द

ये नन्दतनुज! किङ्कर किङ्करं अयि नन्दतनुज मम जन्मानि अयि नन्द

तं मा विषमे भवाम्बुधौ मा विषमे भवाम्बुधौ सदा हरिष्यतिं मा

कृपया तव पादपङ्कज- अयि अयि निमग्नम आनन्दाम्बुधि कृपा

स्थितधूलीसदृशं विचिन्त्यपादपङ्कज अयि अयि नन्दतनुज स्थिते

Darshan

sweet sounds of surrender

MANDALA
publishing group

Darshan
sweet sounds of surrender

MANDALA PUBLISHING GROUP

2240-B 4th St., San Rafael, Ca 94901

Phone (415) 460-6112   Fax (415) 460-5218

mandala@mandala.org   www.mandala.org

©2000 Mandala Publishing Group

Photos ©2000 Mandala Publishing Group

Illustrations ©2000 Mandala Publishing Group,

used under licensing agreement with B. G. Sharma and Indra Sharma.

Library of Congress Catalog Card Number: 97-074368

ISBN: 1-886069-48-4

Printed in Hong Kong through Palace Press International

Table of Contents

Introduction

introduction

USIC IS THE BRIDGE BETWEEN THE INNER AND OUTER WORLDS, between essence and form—subjectivity and objectivity. Great musicians have the capacity to communicate the feelings and visions that capture their hearts and imaginations.

Song is native to our humanity. The ability to communicate our inner thoughts and feelings is the most fundamental quality we possess. We exist to love and share. Therefore, music is not the exclusive property of one sector of society, but a necessary function at work somewhere in everyone's life.

Essentially, sound evolves from spirit. Herein lies the deeper reality of the creative impulse: great works of art are doorways to the inner world. When we experience the contributions of musicians, poets, and painters who have seen through

the eye of spirit, we too receive something of the creative essence that inspired them. Through their work, we connect with the inner reality— Reality the Beautiful.

The music of Rasa invites us to participate in the sounds and rhythm of spirit. As we listen and allow the music to evolve within us, we take part in the creative life of two great artists, Kim Waters and Hans Christian. At the same time, the inspired words of one of Bengal's most renowned saints, Bhaktivinode Thakur, shine through the veil of the world and enter our hearts.

The transmission of spiritual experience is deeply felt through music. The inspired side of the artist is a reflection of the unlimited beauty emanating from the spiritual realm. Here is the place where their inspiration has been transformed into sound and is humbly offered to the listener. We are invited to experience the spiritual current moving through the musicians and receive that endless flow of grace.

Raga & Aesthetics

AMONG THE MANY FORMS in which the human spirit has tried to express its innermost yearnings and perceptions, music is perhaps the most universal. There is something in music that transcends and unites. This is evident in the sacred music of every community—music that expresses the universal yearning that is shared by people all over the globe."

—H.H. the Dalai Lama

The great sages of ancient India did not feel that silence was the final word on spirituality. Beyond shanti (peace), there is ananda (bliss). Sound has always been a path that lends meaning, whether through the telling of stories and myths or in the powerful ability of mantras to connect us with higher realities. Sound and music emerge from the deeper structures of the self. They are abstract and thus more capable of expressing the subtle elements of experience radiating from the soul, such as emotion and wisdom.

Musicians, like dancers or dramatists, are pilgrims and guides through the inner landscape. They are shamans and wisdom keepers who navigate us through the territories of the heart. Journeying through dreams, aspirations and desires, they climb the mountains of the mind and, standing at the overpass, signal us to journey on. Moving us beyond the realm of imagination, they direct us to the soul and further on into the infinite. They aid us in awakening all dimensions of the soul and to a deeper unity with Godhead. Beyond the world of senses and mind we behold with our inner eye a glimpse into the heart of transcendence—we receive darshan.

The idea that song is a powerful tool in awakening spiritual consciousness is not a foreign one. The raga of Indian classical music and its basis in Indian secular aesthetic theory are considered vital in affording deeper self-knowledge.

Raga is the fundamental musical concept upon which the Indian classical music tradition is based. Raga in the Hindi language means "a color," indicating that raga is a vehicle to impress a specific emotional state upon the mind of the listener. The melodic characteristics of a raga, its series of notes and scales, are all employed to communicate the elements of aesthetic experience. The raga is then a vehicle to awaken experiences of what is known in Sanskrit as rasa. These experiences are the emotional prototypes of our humanity. They are analogous to the primary colors, by which all other more complex shades and tones are produced. Thus these sentiments or emotional experiences are the basic patterns and structures of our emotional lives as individuals. We are spirit and not matter; we have the capacity to feel—perhaps the most essential principle in life.

Noted Vaishnava scholar Swami B. V. Tripurari addresses this in his classic work, *Aesthetic Vedanta:*

"Indologists have used the term aesthetics to refer to India's dramatic theory and arts. This is not the same as Western aesthetics, which is a philosophical inquiry into the nature of beauty, a branch of epistemology that questions the objectivity and subjectivity of beauty. Indian aesthetics is, however, about beauty and its truth. Bharata Muni is the father of India's secular aesthetics. His *Bharata-natya-sastra* relates that at the beginning of the Treta Yuga, the second of the Hindus' four cosmic time cycles, humanity began to suffer from pride, and thus the joyful life became mixed

with suffering. With a view to remedy this, the gods approached Brahma, the creator. Brahma then manifested drama, in which all of the arts are contained. Drama and its attendants, such as music, dance, and poetry, were thus intended to edify human society and uplift humanity morally and spiritually through aesthetic experience, which Bharata termed rasa."

There are nine primary rasas depicted in the general scheme of Indian secular aesthetics, eight of which appear in Bharata's *Natya-sastra*. They are: *shringara*, eroticism; *hasya*, humor; *karuna*, sadness; *raudra*, anger; *vira*, heroism; *bhayanaka*, terror; *vibhatsa*, disgust; *adbhuta*, wonderment; and *shanta*, peace.

In Indian classical music, Sanskrit poetics and drama, we find the raga to be the key that unlocks these aesthetic experiences. Swami Tripurari explains the dynamics of rasa in its secular context:

"It is sometimes explained…as the feeling successfully conveyed from the heart of the poet through his mind and words to the sahridaya, or the reader with a sympathetic heart. It is the tangible yet elusive relishing of the arts, the experience of beauty."

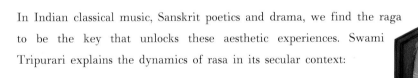

"When we view a dramatic performance, dominant emotions relative to our samskaras [conditioned natures] are portrayed through the characters and various props, as well as through the bodily expressions of the performers. Thus we experience a semblance of the dominant emotions of the characters. When the dominant emotions are further augmented by fleeting auxiliary emotions, the peak experience of rasa is produced within the viewer possessed of a sympathetic heart. Secular theorists conclude that one then experiences one's soul, a unit of pure consciousness free from worldly involvement, yet tainted still by the latent impressions within the soul. This is the experience of secular rasa, which is likened to the realization of ultimate reality by some, primarily Advaitins [Vedantists who accept the absolute to be without form or quality]."

Visionary artist Alex Grey has made the statement "Art is the transmission of states of being." Thus, within the arts, sacred or secular, the goal is to produce an emotional impact upon the audience. The work, whether visual, musical, dramatic or literary, finds its success in its ability to remove the viewer from his ordinary mode of perception to a higher degree of aesthetic or spiritual experience.

Rupa Goswami, a poet and spiritual luminary of the sixteenth century, used the framework of rasa theory to communicate his realizations in the field of consciousness. He saw in Indian secular aesthetic theory a viable correlation to the spiritual emotions sung about by great saints and poets. He received teachings on the science of devotional ecstasy from the legendary avatar of divine love, Sri Chaitanya, in Prayag. His theory is formulated in two works: the *Bhakti Rasamrita Sindhu* and its higher study, *Ujjvala Nilamani*.

Rupa Goswami integrated his spiritual understanding with that of Bharata's secular rasa theory by accepting the eight aesthetic/emotional experiences that he put forth. To these he added four others: *shanta* (passivity), *dasya* (servitude), *sakhya* (friendship), and *vatsalya* (parental affection) rasas. In total there are then twelve rasas, of which the four that express types of personal loving relationship are considered primary. This means that the other rasas are essentially a result of interpersonal love and are experienced through them. Like Bharata, however, Goswami held that the pinnacle experience is shringara rasa, the experience of intimate love. From this one aesthetic/emotional experience all others rasas evolve.

Despite these points of similarity, however, the context within which Rupa Goswami was using this theory was totally at odds with that of Bharata. If the legend of the origin of this theory is accepted—that it came from Brahma, the god of creation in the Hindu pantheon—then the roots of this secular aesthetic theory are hardly different from the ideas of Plato or Confucius, who both saw the fine arts as a medium for social change. They taught of the value of arts in refining character and sensibility in the individual and society. For Rupa Goswami, this understanding of aesthetics is secondary; his rasa theory is based on spiritual love for God.

Swami Tripurari draws out the major differences between the conceptual orientation of Bharata Muni and Rupa Goswami:

"In providing information about the truth that is beauty (rasa) Rupa Goswami differs considerably from secular rasa theorists. While in secular aesthetics, devotion to God as portrayed in drama is not considered to have the potential to produce rasa, Rupa Goswami claimed that bhakti, devotion to Krishna, is the only true and enduring aesthetic experience—bhakti rasa. For Rupa Goswami it

involved not merely dismantling the material ego, as secular aesthetics is considered helpful in doing, but promoting one's spiritual individuality, affording entrance into the eternal drama of the Absolute: Krishna lila. To Rupa Goswami, all emotions other than those that arise out of devotion to Krishna are meaningless. For him, secular

aesthetics has no soul, and bhakti rasa alone is true beauty. Rasa is Krishna, and rasa is the true experience of Krishna."

Whereas the yoga of Patanjali seeks a complete withdrawal from sensual experience (ecstasy), secular aesthetics calls for a full involvement in the more refined emotional experiences of our humanity (rasa). Rupa Goswami extended this ideology to express that neither mundane rasa nor its antithesis—freedom from worldly engagement—were the highest spiritual ends. Neither would he accept the greater awakening within the world of experience as expressed in the non-dual teachings of Zen or Dzogchen to be our highest prospect. For Rupa Goswami, the ultimate spiritual endeavor is to cultivate a spontaneous and divine loving relationship with God—the ecstasy of the soul. Certainly, it is his thought that has brought us from the world of art to the world of spirit.

The Land of Beauty

the land of beauty

IN THE LAND OF BEAUTY "Every word is a song…but it is not a sound from this plane. It comes from some other world, a world that is so soft, so sweet, so heart-capturing. It is a world where correct behavior occurs most sweetly and harmoniously. Every word is like a song. Every movement is sweet, like dancing. Everything is replete with the highest degree of beauty. This is the land where everything has a touch of divine beauty. The Prime Cause is charming, attracting, and arrests the heart and soul."

-SWAMI B.R. SRIDHAR

KEN WILBER, A PIONEER IN TRANSPERSONAL THOUGHT, rephrases the universal question, "Does history, then, have a final omega point, the Omega of all previous and lesser omegas? Is there an actual End to History as we know it? Are we being drawn to that 'one, far off Divine Event' that dissolves its own trail?"

Let us backtrack to the notion of music and aesthetics to see how it guides us toward the possibility of an Omega, a transcendent reality that we can all connect with. How can we further translate the theory of rasa in terms of our individual spiritual goals?

Consider the mandala: it is a symbol for the process of personal transformation and an image of our intrinsic direction toward harmony and the divine reality of absolute love. In simple terms, rasa is that fullest experience of love that comes when we enter into a relationship with the Divine Harmony, the drawing point that seeks our change. It is the nature and function of beauty. Beauty, the highest conception of reality, attracts all and integrates all in its fundamental existence. So as we evolve toward our highest potential, we see that our vision and behavior become more harmonious and encompassing. The dualities and conflicts that arise from our fragmented worldview dissolve as we open to a broader existence in love. This is the move to the center of the mandala of consciousness, into the lap of beauty.

Philosopher sage of the modern era, Swami B.R. Sridhar discussed these dynamics of harmony in this way:

"So what is harmony? How are things of opposite types harmonized by a higher principle? To harmonize things on one particular plane through the energy of a higher plane, it is necessary to harmonize thesis and antithesis in a synthesis: possibility, the possibility of opposition, and then to do away with the opposition. Whatever exists must have its 'anti', or natural opposite. Whatever statement anyone makes, its opposite is possible. Hegel says that to harmonize these contradictions is the process of our progress. In this process, an ever greater conception of harmony is necessary.

"The highest type of harmony is one in which diversity exists. Thus, opposition helps humanity to not only become harmonized, but it enhances the beauty of this harmo-

SWAMI B.R. SRIDHAR

ny...beauty and harmony are the same thing. In this way, opposition ultimately enhances beauty. If there were no diversity then beauty would not be possible."

Rupa Goswami

Here Swami Sridhar indicates that the processes of evolution and struggle that exist in our world create a greater synthesis of love and perfection in ourselves. Our personal progress is seen in light of the higher purpose of becoming part of an already wonderful reality. This Swami Sridhar calls *vilasa*—life in the transcendental sphere, the Omega. Our personal journeys are elements of the wholeness of the macrocosmic mandala, one that symbolizes the universal struggle for integration and harmony. In the center of the mandala is that essential harmony that is the object of all our searches.

"Different things there will be. And they will be harmonized and that is beauty, *vilasa*. Otherwise, everything will be summed together in Brahman, an undifferentiated mass of consciousness. Krishna represents beauty and His harmonizing capacity exceeds and supersedes everything. The conception of the greatest harmony is that He can harmonize anything and everything; there is no contradiction that He cannot harmonize...all is harmonized so sweetly. Beauty means that; harmony means that."

With these words, Swami Sridhar indicates that Godhead is personal. His transcendent personality epitomizes beauty and supersedes His nature as Brahman, formless spirit or consciousness. He is the very heart of existence and love. Krishna represents the highest harmony and the Omega that attracts us beyond time. He is absolutely involved in our journey to fulfillment. The poetry and devotional aesthetic theory of Rupa Goswami pursue this notion of divinity—a loving relationship with Godhead, Krishna.

Love & Creativity

love & creativity

"There is no loftier mission than to approach the godhead nearer than other people, and to disseminate the divine rays among humanity."

—LUDWIG VAN BEETHOVEN

Spirit inspires the soul of artists with dreams and visions for our enlightenment. When such inspired artists offer their insights and wisdom we are nourished as a world community. They lead us to a more whole and spiritualized world-view. They incite in us the drive for conscious evolution. The call of the artist, whether musical, visual, or literary, is to receive these visions of wholeness and communicate them for the welfare of others. As sensitive members of our shared world, we need to be attentive to these messages that evolve from within.

Emerson wrote, "It is very certain that it is the effect of conversation with the beauty of the soul to beget a desire and need to impart to others the same knowledge and love. If utterance is denied, the thought lies like a burden on the man. Always the seer is a speaker. Somehow his dream is told; somehow he publishes it with solemn joy; sometimes with pencil on canvas, sometimes with chisel on stone; sometimes in towers and aisles of granite, his soul's worship is built; sometimes in anthems of indefinite music..."

How do we inherit the power of creativity and love? It only requires sensitivity and a willingness to give others what we have received. This is the progressive intuition that is at the heart of all artistic expression. It is this spirit and vision of harmony that we experience in the music of Kim Waters and Hans Christian. They are committed to sharing these values of love, truth and beauty. Through their gift, we can open the door to the world where beauty and the artist remain eternally in dance.

Bhaktivinode
bhaktivinode

THE MAJORITY OF THE SONGS in this collection were composed by the eminent poet saint Bhaktivinode Thakur. They are prayers and visions of Lord Krishna and Sri Chaitanya. Sri Chaitanya is considered to be the combination of Krishna himself along with his eternal consort, Radha, embodied as one in the form of a devotee. He descended in the 16th century to teach the world the process of chanting the holy names of God and to bestow divine love upon all.

Bhaktivinode was one of the greatest revitalizers of the Vedic tradition, the basis of India's sacred and secular thought. He revered the concept of universal and divine love over all other goals in life and dedicated his existence to sharing his vision with humanity. He had dreams of a world community that would support the spiritual evolution of each of its members. In addition to the large corpus of literary works he produced, the example of his personal life is a beacon of light for others on the spiritual quest. In his later years, Bhaktivinode lived as a solitary mystic. Earlier, however, he was deeply involved in Bengal's intellectual and social networks. His modern upbringing gave him a practical awareness that aided him in expressing his more esoteric insights into our spiritual nature.

Bhaktivinode Thakur was born Kedarnath Datta on September 2, 1838, in an aristocratic family of Birnagar, West Bengal. From childhood he excelled in all fields of learning and displayed an extraordinary inquisitiveness for truth. Kedarnath learned the details of the Indian historical epics, *Mahabharata* and *Ramayana*, by the age of six, and soon after began studying Sanskrit and English. He composed his first poem at the age of eight.

During his primary education, Kedarnath Datta delved into several faiths and wisdom traditions, from Tantra and the various sects of Hinduism to Islam and other practices current in contemporary society. Disenchanted by the hypocrisy he found in many of the traditions' followers and his own inability to find answers to his deeper existential concerns, he moved on to the thought of the West. He scoured the Western philosophical canon, studying the works of Hume, Goethe, Kant, Schopenhauer and others. He also examined the Bible, Quran, and the Brahmo religion. During his years at Calcutta University in the 1850's he was well received by the intelligentsia and his English poems were published in the Library Gazette. He was involved with several forums that met to

debate and discuss the literary work and thought of influential Bengali and European writers. Besides proving his talents as a writer, Kedarnath became a skilled orator.

Kedarnath took up a number of teaching and government posts from the 1860's to 1880's. In these years, he went through some major ideological transformations.

As Deputy Magistrate of Dinajpur, he met a local resident, Kamal Lochan Ray, who impressed upon him the teachings of the enigmatic incarnation of divine love, Sri Chaitanya, which had become obscure at the time. When Kedarnath happened upon rare copies of the *Bhagavata Purana* and *Chaitanya Charitamrita*, he eagerly reviewed them, reflecting deeply on their inner meaning. He was so moved by the depth of the answers he immediately found in these two scriptures that he embarked on a comprehensive study of them. In that same year of 1868, Kedarnath delivered a historic speech in response to a conflict between the Brahmo Samaj, a neo-Hindu movement in

Bengal, and the conservative Hindu population, named "The Bhagavat: its Philosophy, Its Ethics and Its Theology." In this discourse he voiced his discoveries of the universal spiritual truths that were hidden within the *Bhagavata Purana*, a text that both groups accepted as being from their own spiritual heritage. A glimpse of the liberal spirit that pervaded his search for truth can be seen in an excerpt from that lecture:

> The student is to read the facts with a view to create, and not with the object of fruitless retention. Students, like satellites, should reflect whatever light they receive from authors and not imprison the facts and thoughts just as Magistrates imprison convicts in the jail! Thought is progressive. The author's thought must have progress in the reader in the shape of correction and development.

In 1870, Kedarnath Datta accepted the influential posts of Deputy Collector and Deputy Magistrate in Puri, the site of the famous Jagannath temple. It was in this holy city that the legendary Sri Chaitanya spent the last twenty-four years of his life on this earth. Kedarnath was very eager to further cultivate his understanding of his teachings and activities. He became deeply inspired by Sri Chaitanya's universal conceptions of spirituality and underwent a deeper study of the theory of devotion as taught by his direct followers. For five years he remained there and scrutinized all of the major scriptures of this tradition and their commentaries. He established an assembly of scholars inside the Jagannath temple grounds and publicly spoke on the devotional texts he was studying. Many educated spiritualists came to hear his profound insights on the *Bhagavata*.

At this time Kedarnath Datta became absolutely dedicated to the teachings of Sri Chaitanya. Feeling that the dignity of the Vedic tradition had lost its standing in public

opinion, he set out to reform and reinstate it properly. Just as Gautama Buddha radically rejected the socio-religious practices of the Brahminical religion on the pretext that the priestly class was forsaking its societal role for political influence, Kedarnath Datta denied the absolute social status of the Brahmin, as he saw the same signs of misunderstanding in his own times. Like the Buddha, he recognized that the spiritual purity of an individual outweighs his status at birth. Both emphasized the universal potential of all beings to evolve spiritually in this very life.

In 1885, Kedarnath Datta was given the title Bhaktivinode by his guru. One of his contemporaries was so impressed by his extensive groundwork in revealing Sri Chaitanya's teachings that he named him the "seventh Goswami," after the six Goswamis of Vrindavan, a group of Sri Chaitanya's associates who were the principal systematizers of his theology and spiritual practice.

Bhaktivinode vigorously set out to touch every echelon of his contemporary society with the teachings of Sri Chaitanya. He wrote numerous short stories, articles, poems, songs and spiritual novels. Although externally he was a family man and government administrator, he still managed to produce over a hundred books in seven different languages. His life is the perfect example of what a fully dedicated spiritualist can contribute to society, culture, and religion..

At the turn of the 19th century, Bhaktivinode began to take a more internal and exclusive role in his life as a teacher and practitioner. He retired from government service to the ocean-side city of Puri, emulating the mood of his lord, Sri Chaitanya. Bhaktivinode Thakur was moving into an even deeper contemplative life by which he could reflect

on the more esoteric dimensions of devotion. He continued to meet with smaller circles and discuss his insights. He expressed his deep conviction that the intimate worship of Godhead, employing the path of divine sound to awaken transcendental emotion, was the most exalted form of spirituality. In the spirit of the message of Rupa Goswami, he characterized this position in a famous song: "The relishing of poetic sentiments is not the sacred rapture of devotional poetry. Real sacred rapture is found in the sentiments revealed by the purifier of the age, Gaura. Give up the study of all other subjects and worship the moon of Godruma's forest bowers (Sri Chaitanya)."

In 1914, Bhaktivinode Thakur left this world from Calcutta. Bhaktivinode's legacy is his untiring devotion to spreading the doctrines of Sri Chaitanya. His literary accomplishments made the teachings of devotion accessible to the learned spiritualist as well as the layman. Although he translated and wrote several complex Sanskrit texts, he wrote mostly in Bengali prose. As he was sensitive to the needs of the future world community with all the complexities of modern life, he wrote in a clear and simple voice, always remaining comprehensible. In doing so, he served as a pioneer for future generations of devotional practitioners. He laid out a complete system of spirituality, based on divine loving relationship between the self and divinity, which he considered to be the most universal spiritual truth. His shared realizations supply access to the deep unity and subtle nuances of the wisdom traditions.

Bhaktivinode held a deep concern about our spiritual destinies. He saw the need for a fundamental restructuring of the philosophical vision that comprises the general understanding of our contemporary world—what has now evolved into "postmodern liberalism." He wished to inspire thoughtful people to find the need of the heart; he compiled and translated numerous works on comparative religions and esoteric aspects of spirituality. He also felt that ritualistic religion, devoid of the true spirit of renunciation and wisdom, was external to the primary work that we as individuals need to undergo. Bhaktivinode Thakur envisioned a universal spirituality that would shelter all under the banner of divine song. His invaluable service of composing devotional songs, which are lucid accounts of his sacred meditations on the Divine, continues to draw us into the higher world of spirit.

Govinda Kaviraj

GOVINDA KAVIRAJ CAME FROM THE VAISHNAVA VILLAGE OF SRIKHANDA, the home of Narahari Sarkar and many other close associates of Sri Chaitanya. He was born in a family of vaidyas, or Ayurvedic physicians, as the younger brother of Ramachandra Kaviraj, the famous disciple of Srinivas Acharya and friend of Narottam Das Thakur.

Govinda was not himself a Vaishnava in his earlier days, but a worshiper of the Mother Goddess, for whom he wrote many songs. His inner tendency was toward Vaishnavism, however, and one day he had a vision of the Goddess, who told him that without becoming a devotee of Krishna, one cannot become free of material bondage. As a result, he converted to Vaishnavism and took initiation from Srinivas Acharya.

Afterward, he became one of the most prolific authors of Brajabuli and Bengali songs, mostly describing the romantic affairs between Radha and Krishna. He also wrote in Sanskrit, but only a few of these verses have been preserved. The Vrindavan Goswamis, headed by Jiva Goswami, especially enjoyed his songs and gave him the title Kaviraj, or "king of poets," after hearing his poetry through Sri Jahnavi and her entourage.

Songs & Translations

songs & translations

GOPINATH

Lord of the Gopis

BHAKTIVINODE THAKUR

gopīnātha, mama nivedana śuno
viṣayī durjana, sadā kāma-rata
kichu nāhi mora guṇa

O Gopinath, Lord of the Gopis, please hear my request! I am suffering from my attachments, always addicted to worldly desires, and devoid of good qualities.

gopīnātha, āmāra bharasā tumi
tomāra caraṇe, loinu śaraṇa,
tomāra kiṅkara āmi

O Gopinath, You are my only hope. I have taken shelter at Your lotus feet as Your eternal servant.

gopīnātha, kemone śodhibe more
na jāni bhakati, karme jaṛa-mati
poṛechi saṁsāra-ghore

O Gopinath, how will You purify me? I do not know what devotion is, my mind is burdened with greed, and I have fallen into a perilous darkness.

gopīnātha, sakali tomāra māyā
nāhi mama bala, jñāna sunirmala
swādhīna nahe e kāya

O Gopinath, I am surrounded by illusions. I have no strength or understanding, and I am far from being liberated from earthly temptations.

gopīnātha, niyata caraṇe sthāna
māge e pāmara, kāṇḍiyā kāṇḍiyā,
korohe karuṇā dāna

O Gopinath, an eternal place at Your divine feet is what I beg for, weeping and weeping; please give me the gift of Your mercy.

gopīnātha, tumi to sakali pāro
durjane tārite, tomāra śakati,
ke āche pāpīra āro

O Gopinath, You are able to do anything, and You have the power to deliver us all. Who could be more lost than myself?

gopīnātha, tumi kṛpa-pārābāra
jīvera kāraṇe, āsiyā prapañce,
līlā koile subistāra

O Gopinath, You are the ocean of mercy. Having come into this phenomenal world for the sake of the fallen souls, You expand Your divine pastimes.

gopīnātha, āmi ki doṣe doṣī
asura sakala, pāilo caraṇa,
vinoda thākilo bosi

O Gopinath, what flaw has made me so sinful that I remain here in worldly existence while all the demons attained Your lotus feet.

BHAJAHU RE MANA

Oh mind, worship the son of Nanda!

GOVINDA KAVIRAJ

bhajahu re mana śrī-nanda-nandana
abhaya-caraṇāravinda re
durlabha mānava-janama sat-saṅge
taroho e bhava-sindhu re

O mind, just worship the lotus feet of the son
Nanda, which make one fearless. Having
obtained' this rare human birth, cross over the
ocean of worldly existence through the associ-
ation of saintly persons.

śīta ātapa bāta barisana
e dina jāminī jāgi re
biphale sevinu kṛpaṇa durajana
capala-sukha-laba lāgi re

Through both day and night I remain sleep-
less, suffering the pains of heat and cold, the
wind and the rain, uselessly serving wicked
and miserly men to win a moment's flickering
happiness.

e dhana jaubana, putra parijana
ithe ki āche paratīti re
kamala-dala-jala, jībana ṭalamala
bhajahu hari-pada niti re

What assurance of real happiness is there in
all of one's wealth, youthfulness, sons and
family members? This life is tottering like a
drop of water on a lotus petal; so always serve
and worship the divine feet of Lord Hari.

śravaṇa kīrtana, smaraṇa vandana,
pāda-sevana, dāsya re
pūjana, sakhi-jana, ātma-nivedana
govinda-dāsa-abhilāṣa re

Govinda Das longs to engage himself in the
nine processes of bhakti; namely, hearing and
chanting the glories of Lord Hari, constantly
remembering Him and offering prayers to
Him, serving His lotus feet, identifying himself as the Lord's servant, worshiping Him in
the deity form, serving Him as a friend, and
completely offering himself to the Lord.

GAURA-ARATI

Arati ceremony of Lord Chaitanya

BHAKTIVINODE THAKUR

kibā jaya jaya gorācānder āratiko śobhā
jāhnavī- taṭa- vane jaga-jana- mano- lobhā

dakhiṇe nitāi-cānda bāme gadādhara
nikaṭe advaita prabhu śrīvāsa chatra- dhara

basi āche gorācānda ratna- simhāsane
ārati karena brahmā- ādi deva- gaṇe

narahari ādi kari cāmara ḍhulāya,
sañjaya mukunda bāsu ghoṣa ādi gāya

śaṅkha bāje ghaṇṭā bāje bāje karatāla
madhura mṛdaṅga bāje śunite rasālā

bahu-koṭi-candra jini vadana ujjvala
gala-deśe vana-mālā kare jhala-mala

śiva-śuka-nārada preme gada-gada
bhakativinode dekhe gorāra sampada

TRANSLATION

All glories, all glories to the beautiful arati ceremony of Lord Chaitanya in a grove on the banks
of the Jahnavi (Ganges). It is captivating the
minds of all the living entities in the universe.

How beautiful are Nityananda Prabhu on His right and Sri Gadadhara on His left, while nearby are Advaita Prabhu and Sri Srivasa, who holds the umbrella over Gauranga's head.

How beautiful is Gauranga, seated on the jeweled throne. The demigods headed by Lord Brahma offer Him arati.

Narahari and others fan the Lord with yak-tail wisks, while Sanjaya, Mukunda and Basu Ghosh sing for His pleasure.

How beautiful is the music of the conch shells, the ringing bells, and the kartals. All these sounds, along with that of the sweet mridanga, are supremely sweet and relishable to hear.

Lord Gauranga's beautiful arati is captivating everyone in the universe. His face is more brilliant than a million moons, and the forest-flower garland that hangs around His neck sparkles with beauty.

Shiva, Shuka and Narada are speechless in their ecstatic love. Bhaktivinode watches and witnesses the divine glory of Lord Gauranga.

GANESHA SHARANAM
Obeisances to Ganesh

TRADITIONAL CHANT

guṇa gaṇapataye namo namaḥ
gaṇeśa śaraṇaṁ, śaraṇaṁ gaṇeśa

Translation

Obeisances to Ganesh, son of Lord Shiva. I take shelter of Ganesh, Ganesh is my refuge.

Ganesh, also known as Ganapati, is one of the most widely worshiped deities in the Hindu pantheon. He is recognized as the god of auspicious beginnings and the remover of obstacles. Legend has it that the sage Vyasa had a revelation of the Indian epic, presently known as the *Mahabharata*. Ganesh is said to have been the scribe for this work of over 90,000 verses—the longest poem known to man. Ganesh's influence can be seen not only in the Hindu culture throughout India, but in many countries of Asia as well. He has even made his way into the Buddhist pantheon.

Mama Mandire
Temple of my mind

Bhaktivinode Thakur

mama mana mandire raha niśi-din
kṛṣṇa murāri śrī kṛṣṇa murāri

Please abide in the temple of my heart both day and night, O Krishna Murari, O Sri Krishna Murari!

bhakti prīti mālā candan
tumi nio he nio kṛṣṇa-nandan

Devotion, love, flower garlands and sandalwood–please accept them, Delighter of the Heart!

jīvana maraṇa tava pūjā nivedan
sundara he mana-hārī

In life or in death I worship You with these offerings, Beautiful One, O Enchanter of the Heart!

eso nanda-kumār ār nanda-kumār
habe prema-pradīpe ārati tomār

Come, Son of Nanda, and then, O Son of Nanda, I will offer Your arati ceremony with the lamplight of my love.

nayana jamunā jhare anibar
tomāra virahe giridhārī

The waters of the Yamuna river cascade incessantly from my eyes in your separation, O Holder of Govardhan Hill!

JĪV JĀGO
Wake up sleeping souls!

BHAKTIVINODE THAKUR

jīv jāgo, jīv jāgo, gauracānda bole
kota nidrā jāo māyā-piśācīra kole

Lord Gauranga is calling, "Wake up, sleeping souls! How long will you sleep in the lap of the witch called Maya?

bhajibo boliyā ese saṁsāra-bhitare
bhuliyā rohile tumi avidyāra bhare

"You were born in this world to worship the Lord but you have forgotten this and have become lost in ignorance.

tomāre loite āmi hoinu avatāra
āmi binā bandhu āra ke āche tomāra

"I have descended just to save you; other than Myself you have no true friend in this world.

enechi auṣadhi māyā nāśibāra lāgi
hari-nāma mahā-mantra lao tumi māgi

I have brought the medicine that will wipe out the disease of illusion, the Maha Mantra of the Holy Names; so chant these Names right away.

bhakativinoda prabhu-caraṇe pariyā
sei hari-nāma-mantra loilo māgiyā

Srila Bhaktivinode Thakur says, "I fall at the Lord's feet, begging Him to give me the Maha Mantra."

GOVINDA JAYA JAYA
Glory to Govinda, lover of Radharani

TRADITIONAL CHANT

govinda jaya jaya, gopāla jaya jaya
rādhā-ramaṇa hari, govinda jaya jaya

Glory to the Supreme Lord Hari, who is known as Govinda, the lord of the cows and cowherds, Gopal, the cowherd, and Radha Raman, the lover of Radharani.

JAYA RĀDHĀ MĀDHAVA
Glory to Radha and Madhava

BHAKTIVINODE THAKUR

jaya rādhā mādhava kuñja-bihārī
gopī-jana-vallabha giri-vara-dhārī
yaśodānandana vraja-jana-rañjana
jāmuna-tīra-bana-cārī

Glories to Radha! Glories to Krishna, who dallies in the forest bowers, the beloved of the Vrindavan milkmaids, who held up the glorious mount Govardhan. Glories to the son of Yashoda, who brings joy to all the cowherding community and who wanders in the woods along the banks of the Yamuna River.

The Artists
the artists

Hans Christian's musical journey began many years ago in Germany where he began studying the cello at the age of nine. His father was a minister at the Lutheran church in Hanover where he had some of his earliest musical adventures:

"I would sometimes steal the key to the church from my father's desk and sneak into the church to play there at night. It was dark, cold and filled with terror, but the acoustics were amazing. I'm talking about a building in the Neo-Gothic style, big enough for almost a thousand people. So, I would sit in front of the altar, that sacred space, and I didn't know if I was violating God's space or if I was welcome. I loved those anxious moments and expressed my emotions in wild improvisations."

The unyielding urge to express himself led Hans to pick up the bass guitar as a teenager and become absorbed in rock music. When he was 21 years old he decided to move to Los Angeles to study bass at Musician's Institute in Hollywood.

"I played every hole-in-the-wall club you can imagine, constantly playing with many different kinds of groups, from dark and hard-etched bands to folk and performance artists. It was a fulfillment of my dreams because I could do whatever I wanted, and I tried many different things."

Steadily he climbed the ladder in the scene and eventually worked with established people like Robbie Robertson, Toni Childs, Victoria Williams, and the Sparks. But a persistent urge to express his own ideas kept him on the run. "I felt a strong pull toward doing my own music, and since I lived in the downtown LA area at that time, I connected with a cool little theater scene where I could play solo cello concerts that incorporated light projections, dance, and story telling. I really stretched out on the cello, practicing constantly, composing difficult pieces and pushing myself very hard."

These days Hans is working non-stop as a producer, engineer, arranger and player in his studio, Allemande Productions, in Fairfax, California. "I am glad that I can wear so many musical hats—being a player one day, mixing and mastering a record the next, and producing a project the third. For me this is a natural expression of my musical life, and there is little room for anything else."

im waters is a distinguished illustrator and vocalist. She has been singing devotional songs of the Vaisnava saints for many years, inspired by the mystical teachings and rich cultural heritage of India. Her creative upbringing contributed to her career as an artist. Kim recounts her deep spiritual calling as a youth:

"As a child I remember feeling a longing and pang of separation from God—a spiritual yearning. I was searching for answers when I met A.C. Bhaktivedanta Swami in the early 70's. He taught that the perfection of life was to do everything in a consciousness of devotion, to be a servant of God. For a while I was almost denying my human side, trying to be too saintly, too pure. I had to learn to accept my own flaws while still desiring to be an instrument of divine love."

Kim's meetings with A.C. Bhaktivedanta Swami provided some of the greatest inspiration. His teachings gave her the cultural and spiritual context that she had been seeking for her artwork. Her singing took a similar course. Inspired by the musical explorations of George Harrison and Donovan, who at the time introduced their Western audiences to the sounds of sitar, tablas, and chanting, she was irresistibly drawn to the Indian musical culture. Among her noted works as an illustrator is the celebrated *Illuminations from the Bhagavad Gita*.

A.C. Bhaktivedanta Swami

Instruments
instruments

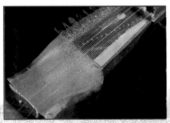

SARANGI–The sarangi is a bowed Indian fiddle with a goat skin top that is played with the cuticles of the left hand. It has three main strings and 36 resonating strings that are grouped into four different tuned sets. Unlike the sitar or sarod, which were played at the courts of medieval Indian nobility, the sarangi is considered a folklore instrument and has been primarily used to accompany singers. Its popularity has declined as the aforementioned instruments gained more and more recognition. The instrument used on this recording was built by Ricki Ram in New Delhi and modified by Hans Christian.

NYCKELHARPA–The nyckelharpa is a bowed Scandinavian key fiddle with four main strings and 12 resonating strings. The player pushes a set of wooden keys that in turn press against the strings. The origins of the nyckelharpa extend back to the Middle Ages, where it shares a common ancestry with another folk instrument, the hurdy gurdy.

SITARA–The sitara is a miniature version of the Indian sitar, with curved brass frets, four play strings, eight resonating strings, and two arched bridges that create the characteristic buzzing sound. The particular instrument played by Hans is custom made from solid ebony by a San Francisco Bay area instrument maker.

HARMONIUM–The harmonium originates in Germany and England. It became popular with immigrant pioneers while traveling west in the US. It was also brought to India by the British. It was quickly absorbed into Indian music culture, admired for its drone quality and portability, but was not considered a traditional Indian instrument. Only in the last century has the harmonium found its way into traditional Indian music.

UDU–The udu is a claypot drum. This drum can be found in different cultures, including African and Indian, and is being made with some variations of design by instrument makers worldwide. Its unique characteristic lies in its design: two openings in a pear shaped clay drum that allow the player to dramatically bend the

pitch of the drum by covering the holes. Some udus even have an animal skin stretched across one of the holes to give them more of a drum sound. A lot of the low drum sounds on this CD were played on an udu.

MRIDANGA–The word mridanga can be translated as "mrid," meaning clay, and "anga," meaning limb. It is an instrument which is constructed of clay limbs.

The mridanga has a very unique history connected to the cultural and spiritual revolution of Sri Chaitanya in sixteenth century Bengal. The instrument is still played throughout Bengal, and there are several traditional styles. These are known as Manoharshayi, Mandarani and Garanhati, and they trace their origins to Shyamananda Prabhu, Srinivas Acharya and Narottam Das. Though the style of playing mridanga has evolved over the centuries, there are still a few teachers who have preserved the ancient traditions without change.

These teachers say that the mridanga, as we know it now, was brought into being when Sri Chaitanya ordered his associates to construct clay drums instead of the heavy and costly wooden drums.

The Manoharshayi school tells the story of Lord Krishna's flute pleading not to be left behind when he incarnated as Sri Chaitanya. Krishna thus allowed his flute to accompany him in the form of the mridanga during his advent as Sri Chaitanya.

CD Credits

GOPINATH
Kim Waters-*vocals*
Hans Christian-*cello,*
sarangi, bass
Greg Ellis-*udu, riqq,*
shakers, shekere
Girish Gambira-*tablas*
Ira Stein-*keyboards*

BHAJAHU RE MANA
Kim Waters-*vocals*
Hans Christian-*cello, sarangi,*
bass, keyboards, percussion
Girish Gambira-*tablas*
John McDowell-percussion

ARATI
Kim Waters-*vocals*
Hans Christian-*vocals,*
vocals, bass, harmonium,
frame drum
Will Windall-*acoustic guitar*

Greg Ellis-*shakers, udu, riqq*
Ira Stein- *keyboards*

GANESH SHARANAM
Kim Waters-*vocals*
Hans Christian-*nyckelharpa,*
vocals, bass, hand claps, frame
drums, keyboards, tambura
Greg Ellis-*udu, shakers, bells*
Ben Mawhorter-*tablas*

MAMA MANDIRE
Kim Waters-*vocals*
Hans Christian-*nyckelharpa,*
vocals, bells, zils,
harmonium, keyboards
John Wubbenhorst-
bansouri flute
Greg Ellis-*riqq*
Ira Stein-*keyboards*
Navadwipa Das-*kartals*

JIVA JAGO
Kim Waters-*vocals*
Hans Christian-*nyckelharpa,*
vocals, bass, drums
Krishna Both-*tablas*

GOVINDA JAYA JAYA
Kim Waters-*vocals, shaker*
Hans Christian-*fretless bass*
loops, percussion, acoustic
guitar, keyboards

JAYA RADHA MADHAVA
Kim Waters-*vocals*
Hans Christian-*vocals,*
vocals, bass, harmonium,
frame drums
Krishna Das-*vocals*
Greg Ellis-*bells, zils,*
shakers, riqq
Girish Gambira-*mridangam*

Acknowledgments

acknowledgments

MANDALA PUBLISHING GROUP wishes to express its heartfelt gratitude to the following people for their help and inspiration:

Bhaktivinode Thakur, A. C. Bhaktivedanta Swami Prabhupada, and Swami B. V. Tripurari, Stephen Hill, Leyla Hill and Jeff Klein at Hearts of Space, Gordon Goff, Jan Brzezinski, and MDG (Mandala Design Group).

RASA thanks:

Their families, Davey and Chris Murray, Yamuna, Dina and Rukmini, Radhika and LiLaLe, John Wubbenhorst, Wynne Paris, Judy Lyon and Stanley Plumly, Neil Greentree, Raoul (Ramdas) Goff, Navadwipa and Sreedharan, Robert Rich, Azam Ali, Greg Ellis and David Stringer.

Author: Hyoun C. Bae

Editor: N.D. Koster

Design: Jonathan Hebel (Mandala Design Group)

Cover Art: B.G. Sharma, designed by Jonathan Hebel

Artwork: B.G. Sharma, Indra Sharma, Kim Waters and various unknown artists

Production Manager: Alan Hebel

Artist photographs and Instrument photos: Neil Greentree, courtesy Hearts of Space Records

Recording and Mixing: Allemande Productions, Fairfax, Ca.

Publisher: Raoul Goff

Also Available
from mandala

ILLUMINATIONS FROM THE BHAGAVAD-GITA
by Kim Waters and Chris Murray

© Kim and Chris Murray

This new, opulent edition of the Bhagavad-Gita, India's great spiritual masterpiece, is truly unique. Profusely illustrated with 40 color plates and more than 50 black-and-white drawings, this volume provides a fresh look at this immensely popular classic. A selection of essential verses is lavishly illustrated, incorporating both Eastern and Western classical illumination styles.

Original Edition $19.95 cloth, 96 pages, 10 x 14"
Miniature Edition $12.95 cloth, 88 pages, 3 x 5"

THE MANDALA STAND-UP ALTAR SERIES
by Kim Waters

Convert any place into sacred space with these gorgeously detailed, three panelled, full-color altars. Light-weight, portable and durable, they make attractive centerpieces for daily contemplation and a splendid backdrop for icons, incense and all articles of worship. Each comes folded, with a decorative ribbon and special mantras.

Devi Altar $14.95, 13½ x 21", Travel size $8.95, 7 x 11½"
Buddha Altar $14.95, 13½ x 21", Travel size $8.95, 7 x 11½"

FORM OF BEAUTY
The Krishna Art of B.G. Sharma

World-renown painter of Indian miniatures,
B. G. Sharma, debuts his lifetime collection of Krishna
art in this stunning, deluxe volume. Within the text,
the artist's mastery and devotion are combined, depicting the magical life of Krishna. From herding cows to exquisite renderings of rasa-lila, the pastimes of Krishna are brought to life with the beauty and charm that only Sharma's unique style can portray. Excerpts from classics such as the Bhagavat Purana and Gopal Champu accompany 180 paintings wonderfully illuminated by Swami B.V. Tripurari's poetic and captivating narrative.

Original Edition $99 cloth, 208 pp, 13 x 12½"
Miniature Edition $12.95 paper, 208 pp, 4 x 4½"

SMARANAM - A GARLAND OF KIRTAN
Agni Deva

Smaranam is a gem with many facets. From its mystical descriptions of Vedic chants to its heart-wrenching poetry and songs, this beautiful CD-book is a must-have. Beautiful photos of India's holy lands and temples compliment exquisite artwork for a meditational experience that seduces the senses. Original Bengali prose with English translations and explanations provide the reader with deep insight into the beautiful and charming nature of the songs, as well as the saints who composed them. Renowned for his sweet Gaudiya style kirtan, Agni Deva sings traditional songs with cross-over accompaniment, making this music perhaps the best yet recorded from this ancient tradition. Instruments include sarangi, tablas, mrdanga, karatals, harmonium, vocals, and sitara.

Item 3017CD $16.95, 64pp cloth, 5 x 5½"

Track list

track list

र्वात्मस्नपनं परं विजयते श्रीकृष्णसङ्कीर्तनम् सर्वात्मस्नपनं सर्वात्मस्नप

नाम्नामकारि बहुधा निजसर्वशक्ति- नाम्नामकारि नाम्नामकारि नाम्नामक

स्तत्रार्पिता नियमितः स्मरणे न कालः भगवन्ममापि स्तत्रार्पिता स्तत्रार्पि

एतादृशी तव कृपा भगवन्ममापि भगवन्ममापि नाम्नामकारि एतादृशी

दुर्दैवमीदृशमिहाजनि नानुरागः तव भगवन्ममापि आनन्दाम्बुधिव दुर्दैवमी

पादपि सुनीचेन तरोरिव सहिष्णुना सहिष्णुना नाम्नामकारि तृणादपि

अमानिना मानदेन कीर्तनीयः सदा हरिः सदा आनन्दाम्बुधिव अमानिना

न धनं न जनं न सुन्दरीं कामये कीर्तनीयः सदा हरिः स्तत्रार्पिता न ध

कवितां वा जगदीश कामये सदा जन्मनीश्वरे आनन्दाम्बुधिव कविता

मम जन्मनि जन्मनीश्वरे मा विषमे भवाम्बुधौ सदा हरिः मम ज

भवताद्भक्तिरहैतुकी त्वयि विषमे भवाम्बुधौ भवताद्भक्तिरहैतुकी भवताद्भ

यि नन्दतनुज! किङ्करं किङ्करं अयि नन्दतनुज! मम जन्मनि अयि नन्द

तत मां विषमे भवाम्बुधौ मां विषमे भवाम्बुधौ सदा हरिः पतित मां

कृपया तव पादपङ्कज- अयि अयि विचिन्तय आनन्दाम्बुधिव कृपया

स्थितधूलीसदृशं विचिन्तय पादपङ्कज- अयि अयि नन्दतनुज! स्थित

विजयते श्रीकृष्णसङ्कीर्तनम्

नाम्नामकारि बहुधा निजसर्वशक्ति-
स्तत्रार्पिता नियमितः स्मरणे न कालः ।
एतादृशी तव कृपा भगवन्ममापि
दुर्दैवमीदृशमिहाजनि नानुरागः ॥

तृणादपि सुनीचेन तरोरिव सहिष्णुना ।
अमानिना मानदेन कीर्तनीयः सदा हरिः ॥

न धनं न जनं न सुन्दरीं कवितां वा जगदीश कामये ।
मम जन्मनि जन्मनीश्वरे भवताद्भक्तिरहैतुकी त्वयि ॥

अयि नन्दतनुज किङ्करं पतितं मां विषमे भवाम्बुधौ ।
कृपया तव पादपङ्कज-स्थितधूलीसदृशं विचिन्तय ॥